FIRE TRUCKS

by Judith Jango-Cohen

PULL AHEAD BOOKS
Mighty Movers

Lerner Publications Company • Minneapolis

E
Jan

Dedicated to the firefighters of Burlington, Massachusetts, who were always enthusiastic about sharing their time and expertise. An extra thanks to Kevin Pollicelli, Kurt Duprez, Peter McAnespie, Gary Arbing, Captain Scott Carpenter, Captain Kevin Browne, and Chief Paul Thibault.

Text copyright © 2003 by Judith Jango-Cohen

This book is available in two editions:
Library binding by Lerner Publications Company, a division of Lerner Publishing Group, Inc.
Soft cover by First Avenue Editions, an imprint of Lerner Publishing Group, Inc.
241 First Avenue North
Minneapolis, MN 55401 U.S.A.

Website address: www.lernerbooks.com

Library of Congress Cataloging-in-Publication Data

Jango-Cohen, Judith.
        Fire trucks / by Judith Jango-Cohen.
            p.   cm. — (Pull ahead books)
        Includes index.
        Summary: Describes the parts of a fire truck, the tools it carries, and the work it helps firemen to do.
            ISBN-13: 978-0-8225-0077-3 (lib. bdg. : alk. paper)
            ISBN-10: 0-8225-0077-9 (lib. bdg. : alk. paper)
            ISBN-13: 978-0-8225-0604-1 (pbk. : alk. paper)
            ISBN-10: 0-8225-0604-1 (pbk. : alk. paper)
            1. Fire engines—Juvenile literature. [1. Fire engines.]
    I. Title. II. Series.
    TH9372 .J35 2003
    628.9'259—dc21   2001004870

Manufactured in the United States of America
9 — CG — 4/1/13

WHEE-OOO! WHEE-OOO! What is
making such a loud sound?

That loud sound is the **siren** of a fire truck.

A fire truck carries firefighters to a fire.
What else does a fire truck carry?

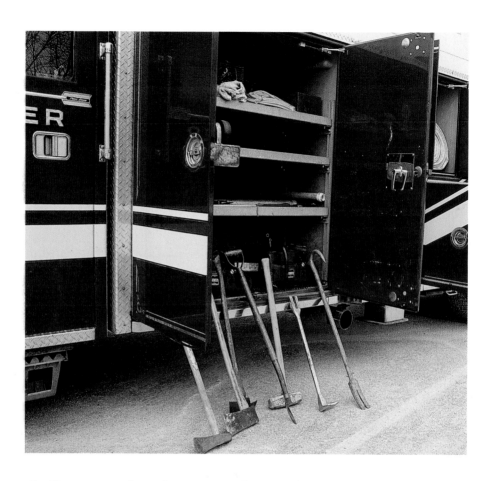

A fire truck also carries tools called **gear.**
The truck is like a toolbox on wheels.

Look!
A house is
on fire!

WHEE-OOO! WHEE-OOO! Sirens
blast and lights flash. A fire truck is on
the way.

Does a fire truck speed away like
a racecar?

No! A fire truck is too heavy to race safely. A heavy truck must move at a normal speed.

Soon the fire truck is at the fire.
Firefighters open the truck's big doors.
The gear is stored behind these doors.

Axes can chop burning walls. **Pike poles** can poke.

The holes they make let out smoke.
How do firefighters work in smoke and
not choke?

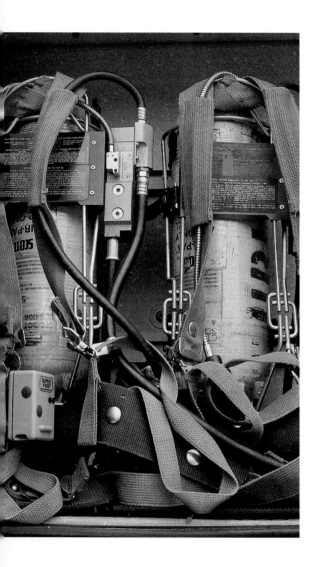

A fire truck carries **tanks** of air.

Firefighters wear air tanks on their backs. They breathe this air instead of smoke.

A fire truck also carries long water hoses. Water flows through the hoses.

SPLASH! SIZZLE! The fire fizzles out.
But what if a fire is up high?

A **tower truck** has a ladder on top. The ladder is heavy. It could tip the truck.

Outriggers must go down before the ladder goes up. Outriggers hold the truck safely in place.

A firefighter moves the ladder with
levers. Levers turn the ladder and
make it go up.

This tower truck ladder is as long as two trucks.

At the top of the ladder is a big **bucket.**
Firefighters can stand inside it.

From the bucket, firefighters can spray
water high and far.

The fire is out. Firefighters drive the
fire truck back to the station.

How many wheels carry the firefighters
and their gear?

This tower truck has two wheels in front and eight in back. Ten wheels move ladders, axes, tanks, hoses, and poles.

This big toolbox is ready to roll!

Facts about Fire Trucks

- Some fire trucks carry their own water in big tanks.

- Early fire trucks were pulled by horses! They carried firefighters and gear in the days before engines.

- Some fire departments paint their trucks yellow to make them easy to see at night.

- A tower truck's ladder can be 100 feet long. That's tall enough to reach the eighth floor of a building!

- A fire truck can cost as much as 40 cars!

Parts of a Fire Truck

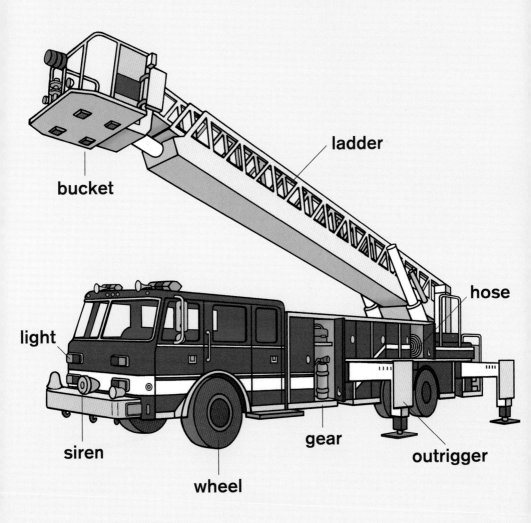

bucket

ladder

hose

light

siren

gear

outrigger

wheel

Glossary

bucket: a place at the end of a fire truck's ladder where firefighters stand to spray a high fire

gear: tools that a fire truck carries

levers: controls that move a fire truck's ladder

outriggers: parts that hold a tower truck safely on the ground when its ladder is up

pike poles: tools used to poke holes in a burning building

siren: a horn that makes a warning noise

tanks: containers that hold air for firefighters to breathe

tower truck: a fire truck that has a ladder

Index

bucket, 22, 23

gear, 6, 11–17

hose, 16, 17

ladder, 18–22

siren, 3, 4, 8

smoke, 13–15

speed, 9–10

tower truck, 18–23

wheels, 6, 25–27

About the Author

Judith Jango-Cohen (center) had a great time writing about fire trucks and photographing them with her husband, Eliot. Working with firefighters Kevin Pollicelli (left) and Kurt Duprez (right), she climbed a 95-foot ladder and rode in the tower truck bucket on top. Even if you are not writing a book about fire trucks, you can visit a fire station. The firefighters there all love to show off their trucks!

gunnison county
Libraries
connect. discover. imagine. learn.
Gunnison Library
307 N. Wisconsin, Gunnison, CO 81230
970.641.3485
www.gunnisoncountylibraries.org

Photo Acknowledgments

The photographs in this book appear courtesy of: © Judith Jango-Cohen, front cover, pp. 4, 11, 19, 20, 26–27, 31; © Eliot Cohen, back cover, pp. 3, 6, 12, 14, 16, 18, 21, 22, 25, 32; © George Hall/CORBIS, pp. 5, 24; © Bruce Gaylord/Visuals Unlimited, p. 7; © Tim Wright/CORBIS, p. 8; © George Hall/CORBIS, p. 9; © Howard Ande, p. 10; © Bruce Berg/Visuals Unlimited, p. 13; © Tom Uhlman/Visuals Unlimited, pp. 15, 17; © R. Al Simpson/Visuals Unlimited, p. 23. Illustration on p. 29 by Laura Westlund, © Lerner Publications Company.